Splendor

Splendor

poems by

Laura Rogerson Moore

Cover design by Shay Culligan
Cover art *Running* by Katherine Rogerson Moore, oil on canvas

ISBN: 978-1-952326-95-0

Kelsay Books
502 South 1040 East, A-119
American Fork, Utah, 84003

*in loving memory of Wayside, whose story inspired this one,
for Katie, who wanted to know what would happen next,
with gratitude, always, for Robinson*

Semper splendor fugit.
—carved into the mantel, Wayside Farm

Acknowledgments

I have several people to thank for their help in getting these poems into your hands: my gifted daughter Katherine for her generous feedback and for her gorgeous cover art; Jonny Gotlib for his amazing photo of her painting; Micah, Nick, Irshad, and Jamie for their praise and swift support, and Shay, Sarah, Delisa, and Karen of Kelsay Books for their careful crafting of this book.

Splendor would not have come to be without the inspiration of two beloved people whose story inspired it. Throughout my childhood, I listened to my father tell stories of his boyhood summers in Vermont, haying on his best friend's farm, and of the girl who lived down the road. When my parents bought their sixty acres up the hill from Wayside Farm, she and the fellow who had lived on the farm with her and her mother for decades helped us cut a road, dig a well, and eventually start to build a house. In my early adulthood, after her mother had passed on, I went to work for the two of them on the farm, and while I will never know just what their living arrangement was, I was always certain of her incorruptible wonder and joy. I have spent the years since imagining how that wonder and joy came to be. *Splendor* is the story of that imagining, and what you read in these poems is invented from the place and what little I knew of the two who lived there.

The years I spent writing and rewriting would not have been possible without the steady and unconditional support of my first reader, my beloved godmother Katie, who passed away just before this book was finished.

And, of course, my greatest gratitude is for Robinson, Grace, Katherine, and Elibet, for their always asking, for their listening, and for their believing.

Contents

Turning Out the Light

Near the end, he speaks of it—his war,
the escapades, the horror—beside
the fire in his Lazy-boy, the lever

slung the whole way back, or later in his
bed when he no longer rises, not
even for the toilet. I hold his

hand, its grasp so ordinary now
as he describes places
I will never go, things I'll never do.

Telling doesn't tire him. Quite
the opposite. He stays awake much longer,
sometimes laughs as I have loved

to hear him laugh. When I lean in to
say goodnight, he thanks me. Then I'm
reaching up, turning out the light.

The Ways of Loving

the way the buck scrapes his velvet
on the sapling, bark
stripping into shreds

the way the borer beetle bites
the fallen branch, softened,
ready for its mouth

the way the bat shelters in a hollowed
stump where she may sleep in
darkness only she can see

the way the wind will toss the leaves,
their pale underbellies laughing skyward
then tangling into calm

the way the honeysuckle climbs,
choking with the breathlessness
of sky's own sunlight

the way the root will sift the soil to sip
the waters, seek the sugars,
clasp the tree to ground

The Latch

It isn't why he stayed or even
that he did. The point is he never left.

The latch upon my door won't catch, and
he never once proposed to fix it,

though it banged in a breeze or swung
ajar. Across the hall, he shifted in

his sleep, staying right there,
right where he was.

How It Will End

We'd always known our story,
how it will end. How to tell
what's not been told before?

The lowering sky is
drenched with mist
delaying darkness.

The pond surrenders willingly to
warmer air, and we might have been
a dream only we were dreaming.

Silently, grackles
lift, blackening
above, turn,
blackening below,
turn, swoop.

Leaves collapse
at the feet of their trees,
becoming everything.

Good Company

O'Ryan cooked the meals—mostly out of
cans, never very fresh—took on the care of
animals, the wash. I ironed, did the dishes.
Sunday mornings, we would change the sheets,
sweep the floors and shake the rugs, dust

if there was need to. Most afternoons, he crafted
picture frames for Daddy's paintings—ones he
selected from the trunk of rolled-up canvas in
his room—while I winged up the hill and waltzed the beaten
paths. When I returned, the daily load would wave

me down to home. He always tucked my underthings
inside his buttoned shirts, as if against the neighbors'
prying eyes as they crept past in second gear.
Each night, I fed the ducks that gathered on
the pond, old bread he'd picked up at the diner

on the highway, what they'd have tossed out
anyway. Mother liked the ducks, their noisy
evenings and the chaos of their dawns. She
didn't like to go in or out of darkness with
anything akin to quiet it deserved,

the rest that it allowed. We never named them
all, but a few did merit that attention,
returning every year, and some stayed through
the summer months. "Why not?" O'Ryan once
did ask. "Free meals, good company."

Before the Not Yet

We participate in
this, in time—the passed,
the moments just

before the not yet

passed. All anyone thinks
they see is what
the light allows, but

even darkness
has its hues.

Home Baptists

"To home," he tells the hospice nurse who asks
him where he worships, and I know exactly
what he means, wandering in a sudden
flight of late spring snow, flakes aslant across my path.

The last time he was on the screened-in porch, he
didn't care about the pollen, only
wanted deviled ham and to sit awhile
on the farther side near the empty pasture

where no cattle gathered anymore, just
a breeze that smelled of boyhood traipsing hills
all afternoon, far from home and chores
as long as he was able. He has told me

of those days—hard poverty, his father's
harder hand, and his mother's sugar cravings,
the music which she beat from out
the ancient upright he would never learn

to play—a hardness of his own, I supposed—
how he leaned against its side as chords throbbed
through him, thighs pressed to chest and hunger
the quiet cave between.

Things I'd Thought I Might Have Lost

Swept clean, stalls shoveled
daily, fresh shavings laid,

the loft stacked high with bales,
their symmetry assuring—the barn

O'Ryan kept just right. I liked
to lie there on the rainy evenings

when the chores were done and day
was letting go, unraveling. The watery

noise beating on the tin above, the lowing
of his cows below left more room for thought.

When I aroused at last, returning to the house,
no one ever asked me where I'd been. Draping

them across my kitchen chair
as breakfast started—more than once—

O'Ryan brought me back
a sweater, scarf, or hat struck with strands of hay—

things I'd thought
I might have lost.

Wild Grapes

Where no one
harvests, the wild
grapes grow,

weighing down
the trees their vines
have grasped.

Breathing in, I
taste their sweetness,
their very own

sweetness leaving me
warmer for having
arrived.

The Boiler

Sometimes, still, I'll shiver when updrafts weave
around my ankles or at those sudden
sighs from a quiet house. O'Ryan installed
the Norge after he moved in, found it at
an auction and had the money set aside
to outbid everybody else, though not
many disputed with him over it.

He spent his evenings building out a palette,
cutting in the vents, and come the first hard frost,
he filled the tank with oil, cranked the heat, and
with a proud and unaccustomed flourish,
invited us to sit to supper.

Its ardent clatter underlay our coldest
months, and every May, he built it all again—
pieces spread across the lawn—until the stillness
of the house became as much a sign of
spring as the clamor of returning geese,
the groan of melting ice, the crack of its
final letting loose the upheld pond, as
reliable as O'Ryan every morning
across from me at breakfast, slurping soft-boiled
egg mixed with shredded pumpernickel toast.

Ice-Out

The pond boomed, shifted, cracked, calved.
The wind howled, battered, bearing
thick chunks to shore, lifting them
into themselves, shoving
the sheet aside, unseizing

the winter-bound water,
and each year we wagered when,
none of us ever getting
it right. Sometimes, he spent
his days away hiking up

the hills onto the mountain
or else on lonesome drives,
unlearning his father's
lessons in love. Once, Mother

wondered out loud if he'd been more
firm with the mother of his son,
but he halted her right there—his
memories as costly as
the absences he harbored,
the promises he kept.

Miles to Go

I hoped for glimpses to know of what he'd left
behind, of why he'd been discarded or
dismissed, for she remained his wife. I knew
he paid the taxes and, some years later, learned

he bought their son a pick-up truck, which
sank, tires deflated, rusting in her yard.
Otherwise, the place was tidy, front stoop
empty, welcome sign upon the door.

Sometimes in early evening if the sun
was sinking low, I saw beyond the black
of window glass reflecting day as lights
switched on, but little was revealed. I never

mentioned that I'd tracked it down and, some years
later, still would pass that way when far up
North on my own, taking the early exit off
the highway, miles to go before arriving home.

A Lonely Place

Landing required flawless timing—the swells,
the wind, the ship, the speed, his hands just right
upon the grips. Take-off, more so. Three years
he flew alone, his ears awash with noise
of flight, radio demands, the quiet of his mind
which talked sometimes as well—a practice for
old age, he said. The clouds provided passage from
one blue to another, holes through which
he climbed—the sky a lonely place. Some missions
lasted days and nights, and once, he lost the ship
and had to land in the Melanesians
on some island where he stayed a week, drinking
rum, eating fish, telling his tall tales. When

he got home to his wife and son, he'd never
wanted to leave the ground again, but all
already to him was lost. His final days,
his gag reflex brings everything back up,
and he loses the moments as they march
across the room or float sometimes or
careen full flight and imagination
has to throttle down until all else is
almost lost, even reason, that nose-dive
into the difference between now and
ever after—hours of feeling like he is
doing nothing, always on the verge
of not doing nothing anymore.

I Do

We'd nothing to blame,
nothing to praise, just this old
easy joy I won't relinquish,
these sedate revolutions—their turn,
turn, turn—everything the story

includes—beginning to end—and
time which already had beyond
us passed—the reasons

we were present, passing
further into time and space,

turning anywhere, blameless, without
praise. What do I want from my

life? I ask myself, "Do you
want to be here?"

I do. Every
day. Blame no one. None praise.

Clean Splitting

Balanced on the ridge between two ruts, I
sifted through a stack of bills, wondering
how we'd pay until an oil truck came rumbling

past the mailbox, parking over by the barn
and out emerged a man who asked which side
the house our oil tank was on. What I noticed

was his sturdiness, a bulk I'd come to learn
would disappear in usefulness and labor.
I gestured round the house where, by the kitchen

door, the wood pile fell well below the sill.
We'd yet to raise it. Dressed in black still, Mother
peered from up in Daddy's room where she'd been

sorting through his paintings since the day before.
Unfurled, their piney expirations traced the darkness
where I lay across the hall in my narrow

bed. We could sell some more of them, we knew,
but Mother hated choosing. More losing
made her cry. "We don't have a furnace," I

explained, and he nodded as if expecting
me to say so. The mud that caked his tires
had sprayed his rig and tank both sides and told

me just how far he'd come to find us out.
"May I offer you a glass of water?"
I asked and led him to the kitchen door.

Three days later when he returned, the sun had
barely risen after hours of wintry
mix. Mother was asleep upon the couch

because she'd never got to bed, unpaid
bills stacked beside her there. Neither of us
heard his coming or saw him park where he

had parked before. What woke us was his axe,
the steady thwack and thunk of clean splitting,
the damp and muddy silences between.

What Remains

O'Ryan and I used to promise—
when we were ready, we would walk

into the winter naked wood and
settle down side by side in the snow

where we would just, sooner or later,
sleep. The trees tell time, he'd say. They

remember, too. Every year, they
wait until the light lasts long enough,

until they know the warmth is here
to stay—what remains, all that here

remains—earth that holds us all in place—
that silent, shifting old container.

Mast Year

Little left to give away, I find, cleaning
out his room. I've waited till well after
he couldn't climb the stairs, having only
ever entered it to gather what was needed
in those final days, and now here's the last

of him—yellowed undershirts he scrubbed and
should have turned to rags long since, socks he had
to darn himself, for I've no patience with
a needle. When I open out his closet
door, fresh tears turn to look at me, astonished—
as am I—by his specific smell lounging
there among the worn-out shirts and shoes.

Outside, a squirrel chides. He's storing his
winter acorns in the nest he's building in
the elbow of the oak—so many nuts to
gather, so many nuts to hide—here and elsewhere.
He will never remember where to find them.

Three-Day Blizzard

He could not keep still, his eyes and then his
hands running over everything, poking,
prodding, sweeping, searching. None of it
was his to have, but he knew that already.

For several weeks, we did not invite him in,
just thanked him at the door with pie, a jar—
pickles, beets, or stewed tomatoes. First time
he sat to supper, the kitchen seemed to
worry. His footfall shook the windows. His
chair scraped the floor in pale blonde lines that we
could see would never leave. Mother and I
were small, and he took up all the space that
we allowed. Soon, he didn't need the asking,
Mother setting him a place each night. After,
he would sit a while until one night he'd come
to check on us through three-day blizzard snow,
concerned that we'd be drifted in or lost
somewhere between the kitchen and the barn.

His truck climbing the hill stuck fast halfway.
So after dinner, there he was climbing
the stairs behind me, headed to Daddy's
empty bed across the hall, Mother watching
both of us from her bedroom door below.

Barn Owls

Carving the air, competing
with the peeper chorus swelling
in the marsh, their darkened sounds

waken me. Such longing,
how it returns to the same
place, in its season. Ghost

owls, Daddy called them, noting
how they'd mate for life. Outside
my window, the moon is waxing

into fullness that will mark its shift to
waning—that measure of the waltz
between two of the planets in the sky.

Repatriation

Live with choices not always yours, sometimes
you have to hoard your equanimity,
like the sun at evening, serving its golden

light one ladle at a time, or the stars
blinking on only when the darkness is
just dark enough for us finally to find them.

Mother figured out who he was. Lists of
returning men marched through the papers, and she
was not immune to studying their pictures,
stories of their deeds, the families they
came home to, nor to talk of reasons for

their strained reunions—herself no stranger
to love's repatriations, not wishing
upon anyone such loneliness—neither

hers nor his inside that metal tube hurtling
through cloud, under stars, somewhere above
targets intended for his destruction.

Managing

Mother and I could have chosen
despair, yet she was the one

who taught me first to see
the thing then the metaphor

for the thing. Perhaps what
Daddy loved about the light was

its predictability—the way
it managed each illuminated

moment speeding past, the way
it managed him. There was

always the this

then whatever I imagined
then whatever I could not.

Round and Round and Round

Turning them right side
out, thrusting
arms inside of sleeves, feeling

what we all felt,
Mother washed our clothes—
a dress of mine, O'Ryan's pants, her shirts.

One day, hanging a load to dry
beside the pasture fence,
she dropped a blouse onto the grass

and crossed the yard toward the shed.
I stepped out onto the porch to see
what could the matter be. The cattle, too,

looked up to watch her pass,
and the router growled without a pause.
All I could picture was O'Ryan

at his lathe, thickened fingers
thrusting whatever it was
he turned. He would not hear

her standing at the door,
watching as he carved that track
round and round and round.

The Way a Heart

I understood.
This was why.

She'd not deny what
she could love—even

with condition,
with contradiction—

what was not
necessarily required to love

her back. This is
the way a heart

moves so steadily,
without destination. This is

the way it seemed to be
happening.

Twice-Falling

Above her smile, Mother's tired eyes swept mine
as she rose up from beside the bed. Behind
her, Daddy's breathing looked more peaceful

than the night before. A breeze disturbed the curtain
by his face where he slept beneath the open
window. I'd enjoyed myself, I said, handing

her the pearls she'd leant, the gloves. The boy
had held me close as he led me round
the room, the music smart and fast. He'd held

my hand as he drove me home. Within my mother's
glove, a reassuring privacy recalled
that afternoon's return from up the mountain—

an exploration cut too short by sudden
storm—the chaos and cacophony of rain twice-falling
from the sky, the leaves, and never reaching me.

The Stag

Head lolling off the roof, tongue bloated,
purple, swelling out its mouth, the stag's black
eyes stared right past mine, and I ran away,
ran home as fast as I could run, but Mother

wasn't there. So, back across the street, the Green,
up the walkway, past the guests and down the
hallway to the office where she looked up
and asked me to slow down. I couldn't tell

her what I'd seen, only what I recalled
of a stag in the woods on a day Daddy
and I had hiked the hill up over the back
of town on the far side of the riverbank.

"Where are your shoes, Phoebe?" She shook her head
and smiled, suggesting wouldn't I like a cake
to eat when I got home, for me to go and find
the cook just finishing up a batch. "But lets

us save it. After supper," she advised
as she straightened my hem and brushed the hair from
my dampened brow. "Smell," Mother whispered then
sent me off, scent guiding me between

the dining tables, through the pantry. I hurried
home, stepping on grass where gravel might have
bit my toes, and put the cake up on a shelf
as I'd been told to do. In among the

parted trees, the stag had paused just before
raising his head and gazing back at us
until he stepped away and left us there, holding
hands. "Godspeed," Daddy whispered as we listened

for the snap of twig, any rustling among
the leaves, but all we heard was birdsong swooping
in upon the stillness we'd become, and I
my beaming, beating, plashing heart, awash

with what? Time will wield its brush and paint in
colors I but half recall and half invent,
according to the day. I'd never see
again without those layers of the after,

the knowing and the not before, textures
thick to thin, scratched then smoothed then scratched again.
Within the realm of explanation hang
these portraits, whole galleries of my keeping.

Evensong

Around the pond, the aspens twirl their wrists, and the music
of their leaves raises that ancient summer song.

Beside the shed, a stand of birch builds its own pale shrine
before ascending into the cathedral of white pine

as bats probe the dark, feeling with their wings, seeing
with their silent sounds.

Tomorrow, I will call the boy whose grandmother baked
the cakes at the inn so long ago. A lawyer now,

he often sat outside the principal's office, never had a decent
pair of shoes, and once I clipped his fingernails

grown long because his grandmother was raising him and could
no longer see. He'll know what to do

now that I am at this final crossroad. Already, the forest is
reclaiming what has always rightly been

its own. Above me, a carpet moth circumnavigates the lamp, little
knowing it is not orienting to a fulsome moon.

As Is

The silence mostly ours, we rounded that last turn
and found the pond, the farmhouse, barn, and woods
tumbling so fast upon the yard, the rest
of the mountain clambering upward just behind.

I rolled the window down, and Mother
switched off the engine, and a second silence
joined with ours until the wood thrush sang and
another answered and beneath it all
cicadas buzzed.
                I was already crawling
out into the vast expanse of shade under
the oak that canopied the house, running
into the shallows, spreading my heart as
wide as it would grow. I turned back to look
up at the hills hiking all on their own, the trees
standing watch, the private paths between them.

Mother opened her door, and Daddy followed,
leaning on the hood, much too frail to stand
that day, gazing past me to measure shadows
along the shore. Mother climbed the sagging
steps to peer in through the dust-streaked glass at
a wood stove, the soapstone sink, its cocked pump
handle, three chairs tucked beneath a table.
Behind me, a green heron shrieked, rising.

Name-Knowing

The whole earth tells stories.
Shale and sand and clay narrate
a bending, declare a gorge, define
a ledge, describe a rocky shelf, a boulder
there where water rolled it high in gush

and sudden freeze. The whole earth
tells stories of such give, such take, such
listening closely, such following right along.

Pathless birds fly and leave not
a trace. Rock is rock, and leaf
is leaf, and what is this? Bones,

flesh, the facts of a life.

Atop a sheep laurel,
the mockingbird will sing
every song he's ever heard,

while at my feet, a maple
leaf's pea green palm
might press upon the muddy shore,

and I will think of knowing
the names of each of these things.

Fawning Season

Their mother trusts the height of hay waving
in the wind, but I've already sold it to
our neighbor who is set today to cut it clean,
wind it into rows to dry before he

bales it, hauls it down the road to sell to outfits
way upstate. His rig is parked along the access
road, and the crows are gathered, hoping for
a slaughter. Soon, the hawks will join them.

The little ones—indeed, I find two—curl side
by side, unmoving as their mother's taught
them. I do not spoil them with my touch
but lift them in my jacket, storing them

among a crowd of brambles underneath the pines.
All day, I will think of them inside their
spotted suits, nose to belly, eyes squeezed tight,
unseen even as they themselves cannot see.

In Other Words

Regina ad templum, forma pulcherrima Dido,
incessit magna iuvenum stipante caperva.
                                    —*The Aeneid, Virgil*

"Miss Phoebe? Line three. Start with the verb."

"She walked, the most beautiful
queen Dido, to the temple guarded by a young
crowd? Or crowded by a young guard?"
Out the window, a jay mocked the blue
that matched its wing, darting cross the clear,
closed glass. "Oh," I raised my head,
"she's disguised as Diana, too."

"Yes, twice in one book. Ironic. Both mother
and lover choose the virgin huntress as their
disguise. Why is that?" Again, the jay darted
past, but I waited for Mr. Groves to answer
his own question, as was his custom to do.
"None dares to violate her sanctities," he
declared. In the margin, I scribbled the word.

"Sanctuaries?" Daddy later asked as we
reviewed that day's translation. Thinning, yellowed,
no longer stronger than mine, his hands shook
above the page. I shook my head, but—so
unlike him—he corrected me. "In other
words," he offered, "honor, dignity, self-worth."

44

Satisfied

The snow softened through the day,
seizing up again each evening
as light retreated till its half of time.

Mostly alone no matter where we lived—
no one to fool with me—I could fool
myself and be satisfied. Sometimes

walking to school, I'd wander
through the neighbors' yards
under their apple trees. Sometimes,

I'd cross fresh tracks. All night,
the deer picked over apples
no one picked all fall. They'd bend

to take in their teeth that
hardened fruit up through the
hardened snow into their mouths.

Knock, Knock

I'd wake to his knuckles' knocking
against the floor beneath my bed.

I'd knock right back then race
downstairs to the bathroom

to sit along the edge of
the tub and watch him

shave. He'd quiz me on my
declensions, times tables.

All that multiplying—
how I loved to figure it!

Some mornings, even years
after Daddy was long gone,

I'd hear again that tap-tap-tap
and have to remind myself

it was just an acorn rolling
down the roof, a branch

against the window-screen,
O'Ryan patching the woodshed wall

gnawed through by porcupines
I would not let him shoot.

Arithmetic

All numbers
divided

by their selves
become one.

A number
multiplied

by nothing
wants nothing,

leaves nothing,
takes nothing.

Kind of Love

Whenever Mother announced
Daddy was not himself, I'd look

to see, but even dozing all day
in his chair by the fire, he remained

as he had always been to me—still,
slender, tidy. I used to pay such close

attention to his fingers, their precise
tenderness—long, lifting his cap

off his head, dabbing a brush
in paint and stroking a color

into shape, into light, turning
a page or braiding my long unruly

hair. He'd ask me what I'd done
that day or what I planned

to do. Then he'd tell me
his own aspirations. Thus,

he introduced me to the purposeful
imagery of the world, as if

the beauty lay in the purpose—

the flower and the bee, the feather
and the flight, the branches and the light—

as if purpose were a kind of love.

Some days when I returned
from school or rambling, I'd smell

Daddy's paints—the solvents
he used to thin them, not the scentless

oils—a whiff as subtle as his
release of time in strokes—

forenoon, gloaming, dusk. In his
favorite book, Merlin lived

backward, seeking what he used to want,
already having what he'd next desire.

Dress-Up

In the mirror, Daddy had
looked backward, crooked, but I

knew to make my name
that way then hold it

up to read it right. That crooked
backwardness was no surprise.

"Two peas in a pod, like you
sprang right out his head,"

Mother said, and yet her church
hat sat too high upon it.

Her fur collar tucked
too close beneath.

Her tea dress draped too
tight across, but I already knew

what mirrors do, and so that day
I asked if I could play.

The Last Bird

The earth
gives its
water

away.
The sky
gives it

back in
all sorts
of storms.

Wouldn't
the last
bird on

the last
branch sing
her last

note,
ready
to keep

singing?

The Strength of Rest

The noise of his departure—lungs,
battling for air, interrupted
by the lengthened quiets—watching

life go. Watching
death stay. Holding

his slender hand
sculpted by a lifetime's
labor at elucidation,
there was always

inexactly
exactly

what I imagined,
what I could not.

Secrets are not lies, Daddy said.
The feathers of a heron weigh
more than all his flesh and bone—his flight
requiring ten times the strength of rest.

Summer Dancing

The pond knotted with the night
as peepers chanted, drowning
out the murmuring

geese settling into quiet
floating. Daddy held Mother
close, or Mother held him

close, their feet following
close as they could be
without touching, within reach—

first his wheezing cough
then his whispered words, her laughter and
a looseness just beyond,

as the Victrola measured out
a melody along with every turn, as I wound
to keep it going round, as the pond

plashed, as another fish threw its whole self
out of water into water over the sky
it kept upon its surface.

Currentwise

Between the branches, birds lift
into air over air, an intake without
beating. Such silence has no name.

The fat brown brook puckers. Below,
the grasses turn, green, lean currentwise.

Across the pond's soft surface,
a heron unfolds his wings, wide
enough for me to lie me down upon.

Every Time We Say Goodbye

"You pick," I said, and Daddy chose,
gasping out the first few words.
When you're near, I sang along,

*there's such an air of spring
about it*—and because I didn't really know
the words—*a present*

*wrapped with string about it. The day
will start to sing about it.* Neither he
nor Mother ever hid from me

that breathless, hollow, blue-lipped
final bowl of him—wrong-worded,
out-of-tune modulation, major to minor.

Splendor

Even absence

has its hue—those many
colors of the distances

between us.

Atop the water,
the ashes film before
the pond tucks them in.

Its surface has upheld
us all, briefly, and
the sky—its blue, its white
clouds—and the muddy
darkness rising up below,

all three—there and there
and there. Semper
splendor fugit.

Winter Dancing

The ice, a thick black sheet, connected wood and
marsh, road and yard. A flurry, as it fell,
powdered right on top. Mother and I laced our
skates and slid from one shore to the next, reaching
every bound atop the water's stiffness.

Figure skating book in hand, Daddy perched
upon the shore, blankets swarming round
him, creating our routines—hand over hand,
crossover, outside edge and in—grapevine,
three-turn, arabesque. Across the frozen
pond we'd glide, not even pausing as he
wound the Victrola we'd set beside him
to skate the two-minute intervals allowed—
waltzes, polkas, great American marches.

Cherry-cheeked and breathless, we danced
till after dark, unlaced our skates, tugged on
our boots and fetched the music home.

Revolutions

And so we rose
each morning.

And so we set
each evening.

And so we wished
for more or

less. And so
we did not

turn from one
another.

Clean Rinsing

Each morning on my way downhill, I liked to
steer by looking in the rearview mirror,
considering what I'd be returning to before
the fall of night—the grove of trees, the path
that wandered through them, the fields along
the road, the wide-mouthed pond, stolid barn,
the leaning house, the woodshop, paddocks, and
the garden just behind the laundry-line full
of clothes a-waving in the rising, rinsing,
rippling breeze.
               O'Ryan taught me how to drive.
That first September when he picked me up
from work, we'd take all the roads on his
delivery routes, double clutching up the hills,
shifting on the way back down. "If you can handle
this, you'll be good enough to take on any
rig just about," he'd laugh. He kept the cab nice
and clean, wiped off the seat. Windows down and tank
near empty, we'd rattle loudly over gravel,
attracting attention we felt we had to
wave to. Mother always used to talk about
the way the neighbors wondered what went on
within our walls—a riddle none could solve.
At home at last, I'd park beside the barn,
greeting Mother with a kiss as she waved
her hand beneath her nose. "You'll have to air
that dress." I'd race to change then hang it out.
While we ate, it swirled and sank as daylight sank,
the rippling breeze rising up to rinse it clean.

The Feed Store Cap

Never pulled the whole way down but perched up
high and flat in front where the feed store label
stretched, O'Ryan set the clasp to fit just right.

Mother threatened to throw it out, had tried
replacing it—on a shelf in his shop,

a full display. Though seasons turn and turn
the pond from a rippling blue-black to sheerest

silver, the trees from full of green into
bereft of all but sky, the air from buzzed

with joyous feeding—breeding—to welcomed
numbing respite, nothing changes. No, not

really. Longing is another room
in which to hide like that other room
just down the hall—being longed for.

Venison

Alone, away from the banging pots
and pans in the yard where Mother and
I kept hunters away as well as

we knew how, he'd lift his rifle, sight
along the barrel, and hold the shot
until the animal returned his

gaze. Then he'd come home the way he'd gone
away—over ridge, through thicket and
grove, under ledge. We never had to

ask him why he considered pursuit
and that brief acknowledgement enough.

He stalked a wildness he could
preserve by not destroying. All
the meat he'd ever eat already

in our freezer. "And besides," he did
once say, "venison tastes too much like
poverty and childhood." No sufferance
for appetites he'd long since put away.

Butter Pecan and Peppermint Stick

The steady thwack and thunk of each log
breaking and falling, a rhythm we did
the dishes to, swept the floor, washed the sheets,

hung them on the lines—by eight, the chores were
done and I was off to work, heading toward
the highway. He stood at the paddock gate

and watched me drive away, having been the one
who'd told Mother I had to go, having
been the one who first took me there. He drove

me past the grocery store, the park and church,
and into the grade school parking lot. "You need
this job, girlie," was what he said. "Now your

mother's done her share. It ain't gointa
hurt you none." And when I came back out, he
was there, his head tipped back against the seat,

his feed store cap tipped down across his eyes.
Before he started up, he dropped his hand
behind my neck, gave a little squeeze.

The ice cream cone he took me for that day was out
of town. Leaning on the bumper, we ate fast
so all that sweetness wouldn't drip out of our hands.

The Principal's Office

They brought me leaves and stones and weeds and,
by the window, built me snowmen dressed in
boughs of pine and useless bits their teachers let
them filch from out of their supplies. They waved
at me from the height of slide, the bar of
jungle gym. I liked to keep the sashes
lifted, even in the winter when the wind

swept round the room and visitors complained
about the draft. The bench beside my desk
held the naughty and contrite, the suffering
and wounded. I peeled band aids for the scrapes,
called parents for the sickness, listened to
confessions, fears, the accusations, their defense
of right as well as wrong. I answered

the principal's telephone, typed whatever
needed typing, pausing perhaps for the
poignant echoes of a Veery bird
exchange, the dee-dee-dee of chickadees
spreading their important news far and wide,
or the four-note song of the mourning doves
fluttering down from the power line.

Divine Language

One afternoon lazy with confessions—bees
in among the holly hocks by the porch and
swallows swooping over water and its captured
sky, their chittering a constant conversation
no one could understand—he told us his
mother used to speak in tongues. We sipped our
lemonades, ice clicking up against the glass,
down to the last diluted drops. "She made me
go to church till I was old enough to tell
her I would not. Put her in a pucker
when I hung up my Jesus boots. I'd not be
getting through no pearly gates."
                                          O'Ryan's
rocker creaked as he shifted to set down
his glass. I leaned back my head and shut my eyes,
the voices round us an ecstatic choir
we did not seek, nor had it come in search of
us. Mother sighed before she rose to clear our
dishes. "Supper will not cook itself," she offered
as she swung the screen door wide, balancing
the glasses on the plate. "Don't forget you
promised me a salad." And we swung our heads
toward each other, each with one eye squinted
shut. "Sunday rules," he heaved upright. "You stay
put." I stretched my legs, suffusing both my feet
with reckless light where shade refused to land,
rolled up my pants and felt it climb my skin
as a beamish sun fell down its afternoon of sky.

Within

We had no need for answers
other than these—moments
happening over and over—

before and now and after
more real than any other

understanding, as smooth and
still and full of grace

as turtles floating within water
we, too, might float within

and keep on floating,
shore to shore, within
the reach of light.

Storm Strokes

Shoving the reeds aside, the wind
sprang out upon the surface of the pond,
cold and fast. It shivered, shocked
the boat, and I awoke to a storm striking hard.

The raindrops punched my shoulder-blades
as I was stroking toward the shore. Once
I reached the house, my skin was shiny
pink beneath my blouse.

Mother watched me soundlessly
through her bedside window. Then I waved,
and suddenly, we found ourselves
awash with glee. Half her face was fallen,

but the other still could manage rising. We
used to paddle out in summer storms
on days the house refused to cool.
We'd lift our eyes up to it, open up

our palms, our mouths. The rain
would tumble over us, and we would think
about our being happy. We were
so very happy.

Particulars

The trees will tell their stories, knowing what
the other trees will need to know. I have put
my ear against their trunks as sap begins
to rise, heard them hum. They understand a thirst
is harder to endure than hunger. Each one

has its mother—enough of light arriving
underneath her canopy eventually for her
herself to replace. Even as she rots,
she feeds the insects, houses birds and bats.
When she topples, her trunk might dam a stream.
And where it pools, the salamanders spawn.

Between a name and story lie particulars.
All day, the hills lift up the trees, and if I
breathe in deep, high up, among the channeled trunks
beneath the widest crowns, I'll taste their ripest
respirations, their purest patience—so green

and oh so blue.

Measure into Measure

All April, the ledges made their slow ascent
toward the spring—the quiet hatching of the trees,
the noisy crowds that thronged them—and I would
search for dry flat rocks where I so loved to lie,

seizing time, home from work. A hawk cried high
while green propelled itself at leaves, which welcomed
time, spilling measure into measure. From down
below, O'Ryan sang some made-up song,

and *Phoebe, Phoebe, Phoebe* came traipsing
up the hill as if to fetch me long before
he'd look across the mud-clogged yard from by
the kitchen door and ring the bell to call me

down to eat my supper, change over Mother's sheets,
wash her helpless half-done body clean, and play
her something sweet to help her sleep, marking time
by tapping on her careworn, calloused palms.

Without a Trace

Head-on, the eagle flew
until it swerved, its great
expanse more visible

in turning, going far away,
like everything—almost and
then not quite

now and then
next now.

What else will pass
without a trace? Look
down. This trail is worn, even

among the brambles. Look
up. What leaves are left are busy
sorting through the light.

Date Night

Saturday nights, we went out to eat—same place,
same things—chicken parm, shepherd's pie, banana
split—food we never had at home. We shared
desert and watched our waistlines, sipping
coffee in between the bites. The nice new waitress
always recognized the two of us. "Date
night, isn't it?" she'd say. To which we never
could develop any adequate reply.

The only time O'Ryan entered my room—
crossed the hall and stood inside the door, watching
me where I sat, my back to him, staring
at the path up through the trees and onto
the ridge where I'd just been remembering
my mother, lest I forgot—I wasn't thinking
about a service, not yet. I wasn't even
thinking much of anything anymore by
then until there he was just standing there.
Even though I couldn't see, I knew he
stood with feet fixed wide apart directly
underneath his hips, hands hanging at his sides,
palms facing back behind. And suddenly,

I was thinking how he might always be
there and that we'd never discuss it. "All set?"
he asked. "All set," he said again. Then he tapped
between my shoulder blades and drew his hand away.

Leaves

The bottom of
the leaf is for
the breath. The top

absorbs the light—
its colors—all
excepting green.

Together, they
becalm and cool
the air, come down,

create the soil.
In times of drought,
all trees agree

to bloom at once.

Divining

The way he told it, the storm was an evening
rumbler. An apple-shaker, he called it.
He'd been at the sink, putting his mouth against
the nozzle, the pump cocked full of prime, when
the house was struck—the tin roof, he thought—
and he was thrown straight back.
                                                 "I landed on
the oven door my mother just had cracked to check
her cakes. She yanked me off, not so's I wouldn't
burn. To save her sweets, sugar coming dear that
year. All she said was served me right, drinking
from the spout." And this, he claimed, the reason
he could locate water without a dowsing rod, afoot
in neighboring fields or in a parking lot, and once
an auction to which he'd taken me, hoping to find
a boiler part.
                                 He'd shiver. "Here," he'd say, stopping,
standing, still. Somewhere deep beneath our feet, that
revelation pooled—so secret, ours, and bedrock-bound.

Only Blue

Like a certain friend, the pond nudges
my back where it rests against the skiff's
flat bottom as air tiptoes across

its soft surface. Above me, the sky
is only blue and I just
in the very middle for

the moment when the tree-tops
lean in to look—feet dangling
over the gunwales, gathering

the light between my toes
until the breezes comb them out
and I wonder about breakfast,

what I'll feed myself today.
Paddling back to shore, I wave
to the paper boy pedaling past.

By Heart

Over her back, the doe meets my gaze,
neck long and curved, tail flicking at flies—
its white a kerchief she waves, not an
alarm, revealing the perfect pink

swell of her udder. She's here for the early
apples fallen hard and green in under
the low-hanging branches of the trees,
her fawn somewhere nearby, lying low.

A goldfinch swoops above my head from off
the mantel where I've scattered seeds, its
syncopated song cascading in
its wake. By day, I keep the doors and

windows open so birds can fly inside
and out as long as I'm still here
insisting on that ancient verse I
know by heart—I am—still wondering

how the final notes can have no such
refrain. By night, I stretch out in
the yard, attending to the constellations
scrolling down the pages of the sky.

About the Author

Laura Rogerson Moore lives in New England with her husband. She teaches writing and literature. *Splendor* is her third book of poems.